Who Does God Say You Are?

Amayah Shantel Smith

Who Does God Say You Are?
Copyright © 2020 by Amayah Shantel Smith

All rights reserved. No part of this book may be reproduced or transmitted in any form or by any means without written permission from the author.

ISBN: 978-1-7331258-3-3

For More Info visit www.apartofchrist.com

Table of Contents

Acknowledgments 5

Introduction 9

The Beginning of Insecurity 10

A Lack of Confidence 17

Wounded Heartbreak 24

A Renewing of The Mind 32

Coming into A New Image 39

Knowing Who You Are in God 43

Knowing Who God Is 48

A New Truth 53

Conclusion 60

Acknowledgements

For starters, this book would not have been written if it wasn't for God's purpose concerning my life. I want to thank my Heavenly Father, for transforming my life. For as long as I could remember, I felt like I would always live a lost, confused and mediocre life. My life experience hasn't been the most comfortable, but I can testify to God's word in Romans 8:28 that in all things God works for the good of those who love Him, who have been called according to His purpose. I've gained much of everything I lacked in God and I couldn't be happier. I'm still in awe at how good He has been to me, still amazed at how much He has brought me through. He has added more value to me and gave me comfort that I've been searching for; that I needed. I am grateful that I am not defined by what I've gone through. That I am not defined by a status or persona that this life gives but defined by the Word of God. Thank you, God, for all you have done for me and for making this moment in my life possible. Let my life be for your glory.

    To my Mom who is my biggest support system. Thank you for always believing in me when I hadn't believed in myself. Thank you for your unconditional love, for your wisdom and your guidance that has motivated and inspired me to grow closer to God for myself. You are the game-changer in our family, the one I adore, the one who has given me the best blessing in the world—which is introducing me to God. I will never depart from what you have instilled in me. Mom, you are one of my greatest blessings from God, and without your help in counseling me through life, I don't know where I'd be right now. No words will ever be enough to express how much I appreciate you. Thank you for every sacrifice and for pushing me into my full potential. Nothing you do for me is overlooked. Thank you for trusting in God and for your prayers over my life and my siblings'. You are my Super Woman. You are my role model. I hold everything you've ever taught me close to my heart. I love you more than I can truly express. My beautiful lady, you are a joy to my life. I pray that God continues to bless you all the days of your life.

      Apostle Winston Cooper and Professor Jessica Cooper, you both have blessed and added so much to not only my Mom's life but mine as well. You both have stretched me and have birth in me a stronger desire to pursue all that God has for me. Thank you both for seeing so much in me, for the knowledge and kingdom principles you share throughout the week. You two are truly a power couple and I admire your hard work and dedication. I admire your success and your wisdom of helping others grasp all that God has for them. Thank you for making the *Mouth of God Ministries* home for me and my family. I have been truly blessed to be a part of a church family that allows people to go forward in their full potential. I am grateful to have you both as my spiritual parents and I pray that God continues to bring you both increase toward your vision.

To my church family, being surrounded by Entrepreneurs and Authors, Christian Counselors and Therapists, you all have given me so much to look forward to in God. The wisdom, the love, the laughter and the sense of belonging that I feel when we're in fellowship with one another increases my own passion. You all have many gifts in God, and I am amazed at how well you all use them. I love each one of you because not only do you all put God first in everything, but you all have strong faith and believe the manifestation in for your life and your businesses. You've shown me that even when times get hard, there is strength and blessings in the pressing.

    To Elder Jason Hart (although you are a part of my church family), thank you for being someone I can confide in; someone I can trust. You are truly like a father-figure to me. I have so much gratitude in my heart for you. You have always listened, you've cared, and you've been patient and understanding. I appreciate you for the wisdom you've shared with me and for the comfort that you've always given me. You have made it easier for me to be vulnerable and open. You've made me feel like I had a voice after being silent for so long. Thank you for being who you are. I love you and I am praying that God blesses you and your household.

To Kevion, thank you for allowing God to use you in a moment where I felt like He had forgotten about me. Thank you for making me laugh, for admiring me, for being considerate and honest, and for always making me feel comfortable. You were an angel to me, and you still are. I may have not known it then but now I understand that God does things for a reason. He had a purpose for putting you in my life. You have such a great spirit and I am praying that God adds to you as you've added to me. You were my reminder that God cares for me, that He listens, and that He was working things out for me in his timing. You've played a major role in God's healing for me and you were most definitely a representation of an answered prayer. I appreciate you and I love you, always. Last but not least, to everyone God has placed in my life, whether it was for a lesson or a blessing, thank you all for sharing moments with me and being a part of it. To those who've uplifted and inspired me in more ways than one, those who've seen nothing but greatness in me, those who've noticed my strengths and helped me with my weaknesses, those who've been there to give me encouraging words, those who've added to me, those who've prayed for me and spoke good things into my life, thank you. You all are appreciated, and I am praying that God meets your needs just as He has met mine. I Speak nothing but blessings and favor on you!

Introduction

This book wasn't written for self-pity but to share a personal experience that I was once embarrassed to talk about. This book was written for the girls who've felt lost, empty, and broken mentally, emotionally, and spiritually. To help girls find healing, identity, comfort, stability, joy, hope, freedom and sanity; to help them find faith, strength, confidence and power in God. This book was written to help every girl take her authority back.

I pray that this book not only gives them a hunger to know more about God but know more about themselves in God; that it shatters this mundane persona of the world, people, and themselves and replace it with the image of God and who he created them to be.

To girls who have gone through or is experiencing depression and hasn't yet found their healing, this is for you. To girls who have wanted to give up, who have cried themselves to sleep, and stopped themselves from eating because they've felt unworthy, this is for you. To girls who are in a constant fight with their mind, girls who are trying to find themselves, those who wear masks to hide and suppress their feelings, this is for you. To girls who've felt hopeless, devalued, silent; to girls who lost their comfort, their peace, their strength, their faith… this is for you. To girls who have felt disappointment, betrayal, rejection; to girls who felt alone, unnoticed and unimportant, this is for you. God *loves* you and I love you.

The Beginning of Insecurity

Sometimes, when you experience traumatic and horrible things, those things begin to taint your character. Somehow, you allow those situations to shape you into a person you no longer recognize, changing the way you view who you are or the way you view your life. Often, you'll find yourself interpreting those things into an image that is not necessarily real. You might find yourself having a conversation with someone, and when asked why you do the things that you do, your response might always seem to be *"I went through _____ and that made me who I am."* I think it's funny, though, how the world shows us this flawless lifestyle along with a standard of the person it wants us to become. And it's even funnier—yet terribly sad—how we've pushed ourselves to conform with a path and this self-image that God never intends for us to affiliate ourselves with in the first place. You may feel like you must act a certain way that'll diminish your character, or that you have to say things out of the norm for you to be accepted. You may feel like you need a group to push you over the edge, or that you need to be with someone who *makes* you complete. But honestly, no one or nothing can make you complete, except God. I learned this.

    I wanted to find a path well suitable to every aspect of what makes me human —my physicality, my mentality, my emotions, my spirit. I wanted to be more than just this bubble I submitted myself to. No one ever imagines their life falling apart, nor do they imagine being in a place where they'd forget who they are or what makes them as a person. No one wants to feel like they aren't good enough for someone or to feel like the rut they are in will last forever. We never picture ourselves feeling like a lost cause or that things will never turn out alright in the end. We never want to feel like life is entirely *purposeless*. I found myself, eventually, become severely blind and misled by this portrait that the world painted, the opinions of other people, and by the things I thought were true about myself.

    When I became unfamiliar with who I was, I was desperate to seek my identity in things that I thought made me the happiest. I wanted validation, and I wanted clarity; to feel like I wasn't *just living*. Life became constant cycle of me falling and standing back up again, experiencing things I had never known I would, struggling, or going through a battle (whether it be mentally, emotionally, physically, or spiritually) that drained my well-being. The fight I never seemed to be able to win had always been in my mind. There was this exhausting game of tug-of-war and me trying to pull myself out of the old pattern of thinking. I wanted to make my mind a safe place for me, but it always yanked me back into a nightmare that I couldn't get out of. I was afraid of allowing myself to process my thoughts, and that was a big problem for me. On a number of occasions, I tried to escape what was keeping me bound; but without confronting the root of why I was stagnant in the development of loving and accepting myself, I started to become comfortable in the situation that I was in.

Growing up, I was shy, and to be honest, I loved being that way. I was uncomfortable with letting my voice be heard as I felt like I didn't have one. I was trapped in this shell because I felt most protected there; I felt hidden. I felt relieved that eyes weren't on me the majority of the time. I allowed this shyness to become who I was; I allowed it to hold me back, to make me afraid, to become a label that made me restrain myself from opportunities and people. I identified myself with a word that had given me anxiety when it came to introducing myself to others, afraid that they'd notice all my flaws and taunt me for them. Because of this, I learned to cope with keeping my emotions in and hiding it behind a smile when internally, I was crying out for help. Now much older, I've realized that I was suffering from identity crisis. I've never found the strength to let go of. If I'm totally honest, the thoughts that I had about myself, I felt like they defined who I thought I was and who I was going to be perfectly.

I developed feelings of disgust and hatred in my heart because of the way God made me, because of this, I became extremely insecure. I was introduced to comparison when I became more pleased with my youngest sisters outward appearance my own. There were things about her that I wished I had, and although it seems a lot odd, to me, she was *perfect*. Although we are different people with completely different callings, personalities, and gifts, I overshadowed things she was good at and dimmed the light on me. There were moments when people would praise her for her beauty and call her pretty or gorgeous and when eyes laid on me, they'd faintly say that I was cute. Eventually, I started to feel out of place. There was this instant desire to be more than just cute. I wanted to be beautiful. I wanted to feel wanted and loved by someone. I wanted to fit in the same category as her.

    I wanted acceptance and reassurance that I was more than what I felt during that time. I hated the color of my skin, and the comparison towards my sister developed strong spite, not only towards myself but towards her as well. I felt ugly. From then on, it became harder to accept who I was, and my low self-esteem got worse over time. All three of my sisters have a fairer tone of skin than mine, I didn't feel as beautiful, and it made me think less of myself and more highly of them. I was wrapped up in the thought that the color of my skin made me unattractive because more boys found their preference in lighter skin-toned girls. To be honest, when it came to be chosen by someone of the opposite sex, that was the real reason I had hit rock bottom.

    I listened to the voice in the back of my head that kept telling me I had every right to feel the way I did. That voice told me I was full of mistakes, that I would never amount to anything, but I had kept telling myself that I would. Every whisper I heard, I believed. I never took the time to think about God or who He said I was, and that is why I ran with what I always thought was true. I didn't know Him for myself. I submitted myself to things like **"*you're not beautiful*"** or **"*you'll always be ugly,*"** and **"*you're worthless.*"** I didn't realize the things I told myself were lies from the enemy.

    I hadn't known during that time, that me believing everything that was going through my mind would horribly affect my communication and my relationship with my family and my friends. Things started to go downhill for me mentally, and I was sure that I was going to be stuck there for a very long time. The feelings that I've developed from the false truths I told myself kept me silent, confused, deeply hurt, and emotionally damaged. That insecurity was a blockage, keeping me from the knowledge of God, and of all He has called me to through His Word. What I've learned, though, is that your imperfections make you who you are. They are the things that God loves most about you, the things that make you stand out, that makes you unique. No one is perfect. God made you just the way He saw fit, and that is enough for you to know that everything in his eyes is indeed, beautiful.

    The voice in your head that makes you doubt, or question your beauty, or make you fearful of being who you are in Christ is the voice of the enemy. As much as I would like to tell you that it is easy to develop strong self-love, it is a struggle. You must be willing to accept things that are difficult to accept; you must be comfortable and secure in how God has made you. I had to write out the things that stuck out most to me; the things that I loved about myself. Doing so allowed me to remember things that are a part of how God made me. I had to write out the things that I liked and disliked about my image, and in the end, the good things outweighed every bad thing that I blew out of proportion. It opened my eyes to focus on the things that mattered, and it slowly but surely helped me analyze the lies that I've believed from the enemy and myself.

    It made me not only see the beautiful parts that make me human, but it also allowed me to find peace with the imperfections that I have externally and internally. No matter how many times the word beautiful hasn't been said to you or the many times you may have looked at yourself in the mirror and saw everything else but beauty, it never changes the way that God feels about you, nor does it change the way He sees you. All that you are and all that you can be is because of God. His word tells you so much more about yourself than anyone else ever could. It doesn't matter who doesn't find you attractive; it doesn't matter how you were rated on a scale of 1 to 10, you are beautiful, nonetheless, and you are wonderfully made.

Points to Ponder:

1. That voice in your head that makes you feel unworthy or makes you view yourself contrary to who God says you are is from the enemy. DO NOT believe him. He is the Father of lies.

2. Turn to God, study His Word, and pray that you will take on the image of Christ and not of yourself.

3. Your imperfections make you who you are.

A Lack of Confidence

When there have been words spoken to bring down your self-esteem, everything in life will be looked at from a different perspective, and eventually, you'll live yours based on the weight of those words that were said to you. Confidence is a self-assured feeling when it comes to things about you like your ability, your quality. It's a feeling of being comfortable with yourself. It's the feeling of being able to be bold and straightforward when it comes to things that you believe in and things you believe about yourself. It's the feeling of not being afraid to step out of your comfort zone to do something outrageous yet spectacular, a feeling of just being free in being YOU.
I never had confidence because I was never fond of the idea of being comfortable with being uncomfortable. I never wanted to step out of that shell I kept myself in, to do or say anything I didn't feel gave me the security that I needed. Honestly, that was another reason why I never had that boldness. I wasn't secure with who I was, and I never felt safe being me. I became fearful of how I was viewed at or what would be said if I became free in my personality. I lacked confidence, constantly reminding myself of things that did not align with who God has called me.

My siblings and I had moments where we'd say things about each other because we wanted to be funny and we wanted to have *fun. We* said things like "you're ugly," "you're stupid" or "you're dumb" just for laughs without the intention of verbally abusing the other.

Nothing about what we spoke over each other was fun. We hadn't realized during that time that words could badly affect the way someone sees themselves. The words "you're ugly", were the only ones that had stuck to me. Maybe it was because I had already thought that of myself, or perhaps it was because my siblings deep down believed that about me as well. When it ran through my ears, I laughed it off because, during that time, those words were nothing but words to me. However, as time went on, it became something I believed more every day. When I looked in the mirror, I was so uncomfortable with staring back at the reflection. I had no confidence. I had no belief in who I was and what I was gifted to do or what I could be capable of doing. I was focusing more attention on things that made me devalue myself. I couldn't accept the way that my body was formed or the way that I smiled. I didn't want to. I started having trouble staring at myself in the mirror for long periods of time or walking with my head high because I was ashamed of being this *ugly* girl. I had anxiety over the thought that I was always being talked about.

Three years ago, in Dallas, during the summer with my sister, we attended a conference that had discussions on the topic of how we felt about who we were and how we felt about our self-image. There was a darker complexion woman who spoke, and I remember her expressing these words: "When I was growing up, I'd always have trouble accepting the skin that I'm in because I have a sister who's lighter than me. I'd look at her and think that she was prettier because she was like this model type, and I just felt like the smart girl."

Her statement reflected the way I had been feeling, and I left that conference hurt and bitter. It wasn't what she said that made me this way, but it was the recall that played in the back of my mind, reminding me of something that I felt guilty of feeling. I started to push my sister away from me because I felt horrible on the inside. I was so angry that I took it out on her, and nothing of what I was feeling had been her fault. I became this mean and distasteful human-being, so torn apart that my attitude changed drastically. I was upset at myself, at my image, at God, at life. During that time in my life, my relationship with God wasn't something I tried or wanted to build. There was no genuine foundation that I've built according to His word or of who He is in my life. There was no intimate moment of expression towards Him, no acknowledgment or adoration, and no worship given for what He's done for me. I felt like I could live this life on my own, and that kept me from surrendering my entire being to Him. I was selfish and ungrateful because I took my emotion out on not only Him but my sister as well. That attitude hindered me from stepping into His presence. I was this backslider who always had Him on the back burner and only called on His name when it was convenient for me. I didn't know what it meant to be intimate with Him, and I never really grasped an understanding of how important it was to form a relationship with Him because I didn't make Him my *priority*.

I sulked in this sadness, entertaining thoughts I've already had in my head based on an idea of who I told myself I was and what I've told myself made me. I never had a yearning to learn God's truth; instead, I lived by what I thought was my own. I lived by assumption, lies, and words that never fell in line with God's word concerning me. I never tried pursuing God because—to be transparent—He had been the last thing on my mind. I wanted nothing but to have my life figured all out, and when I realized that was never going to happen, I shut down and became discouraged. I gave myself poor judgment and believed everything that had been said to me; everything that I've said to myself. I lived up to an expectation that I had to be perfect to be accepted by my family, my friends, people, and society. I created my self-image based on negative words, and those words determined how I viewed myself and how I'd speak over my life.

My confidence deteriorated, becoming shattered. I started to dress exactly how I felt, and the outcome of that kept me stagnant in a damaged emotional and mental disposition. I had no energy to fix the issue nor put effort into making myself look elegant. I had completely given up on the idea of looking pretty because I didn't feel like that would have made a difference if I didn't believe that I was myself. I was afraid of failure and not being the best me. I had a hard time standing up for myself, which always made me feel as though I was weak. I simply just felt like I wasn't good enough. I felt like there was no hope for me. I felt like nothing was ever going to change and that I was going to be exactly how I felt, how I looked, and how I thought.

Your lack of confidence may have you in fear of failing a test or may make you feel as though something is too complicated for you to understand or too hard for you to overcome. Your lack of confidence may have you question what you're able to do, or it may make it hard for you to believe that you are more than what and who people say you are. However, in Philippians 4:13, the scripture tells us that you can do *all* things through Christ, who strengthens you. When you realize that God gives you the strength to do all things and that He is the God who gives you the power to conquer anything that you face, your confidence in Him will grow. Your confidence comes from God. In Jeremiah 17:7, the Bible says, "But blessed is the one who trusts in the Lord, whose *confidence* is in Him" (emphasis added). And when it comes to that time to face a certain obstacle in your life, or to take that test, you'll be able to say "Because I know that my strength comes from God, and because I trust Him enough to stand firm and remain confident in Him, I *can* do this. I *will* do this." Trust in the abilities and the gifts that God has given you. You must keep in mind that the things that you are great at could be something that someone else is not willing or hasn't been gifted to do.

I've come to learn that the truth is we are not to have confidence in anything apart from God. I've learned that no matter what might've been said about me, or how many times I've felt like I wasn't good at something, trusting God not only builds my confidence but allows me to be okay with how well I am able to do something someone lacks the ability to do. My confidence in God (when I later began to build a relationship with Him) helped me to be confident in myself; it made me become aware of being able to look in the mirror and be happy with what I saw. You may feel intimidated by those who have the same gift as you, but I've gained wisdom, understanding that although someone shares the same gift as you (take singing for example), and you may feel like your voice isn't up to par with someone else's, that does not mean that you are no good at what you do.

The same applies to the way you look. Everyone looks different, sounds different, thinks differently, grew up differently, and etcetera. But that does not and will never affect that which God has said in His word about the girl He created. You have so much in you that God wants to reveal to you, so much more than just the surface that you're fixating your focus on. He wants you to trust Him, to be free in Him, to be bold and confident. You are nothing like everyone else, and that is what makes you *special*.

Points to Ponder:

1. Your confidence comes from God.

2. Jeremiah 17:7 - "But blessed is the one who trusts in the Lord, whose confidence is in Him."

3. Philippians 4:13 - "I can do all things through Christ who strengthens me."

Wounded Heartbreak

When I first started my journey through High School, I was nowhere near familiar with getting to know a boy in hopes of thinking it would turn into something more than just a friendship. During my sophomore year, I met someone through a mutual friend at the time, and when we started talking and getting to know each other, I started finding Him attractive. He was sweet, funny, and honest (so I thought). He said things to me that fed my flesh, told me things that I wanted to hear, and led me on to believe that I was who he wanted. He was the first boy I ever really expressed my feelings with (those feelings of the way he made me feel and how my affection toward him was eventually growing). He was the first boy I had ever taken a liking to, the first to make me feel what some people call lovesick. What I thought was love, was far from that.

    I didn't know what I was getting into until I was constantly draining myself, trying to find ways to have him acknowledge me, not knowing that I had no clue of who I really was. I questioned myself, *"Am I good enough?" "Am I worth it?" "Is something wrong with me?"*. He ended up choosing someone else, when he lied, laughed unapologetically in front of me as if I were a joke to him, and rubbed what he did in my face, that was when I went into a long season of depression. It was the first time I've felt deep pain. It was a horrible feeling seeing someone who treated me poorly, treat someone else entirely better. It wasn't because of jealousy, but the fact that I was willing to do anything for someone who never had the intention of treating me right in the beginning, and then seeing that he was cable of doing it all along but just not with me was heartbreaking for me. Every insecurity that I've had, every thought held captive in my mind, I shut myself out from everyone I was close to and everyone I loved. I constantly lost my appetite, struggled with insomnia, went into isolation, and even contemplated suicide. The passion I had before I met him faded, and I found no value in life. I went through this experience alone because I felt I could handle it, and to be honest, I didn't want my mom to carry a burden she didn't create. So, I kept it to myself and lived my life falsely as if I was happy when I wasn't.

    Heartbreak is one of those conversations that we find too hard to talk about because no one wants to remember a time when they've felt unappreciated or unloved. We don't like to recall moments when we felt like we were the problem or that our insecurities caused someone to decide to choose someone else. We don't like to feel rejected, incapable of being enough, unworthy. If you've ever gotten your heart broken by someone you had potential in, someone you've seen yourself being with and felt like you were the problem, I am here to tell you that there is *nothing* wrong with you. You are not the reason why it ended, nor are you the reason why he became interested in someone else.

For so long, I wanted someone to recognize me, to love me, to accept me, and to value me. For a moment, I thought I found the person who would, but all along, I had fallen for a personality and sought out love in the wrong place. I was damaged, broken, confused. I had so much animosity and a desire to hurt him just as much as he had hurt me. There was a shift in the wrong direction of the way that I saw people (particularly boys), and it made it worse for me when I wanted to change the way I saw myself. This fear in me grew when I felt that there will never be a time when someone would accept and love every part of me; that someone would notice my *existence*. Sure, I was noticed, but there was a feeling in the pit of my gut that no one truly saw me for me. But the question I had to ask myself plenty of times was: *Do I really know who I am?* Most times we try so hard for someone to know us and to love us when in actuality, we have no clue who we are and we have no self-love (which does not always have to be about loving who we are and how we were made but also about lowering our standards for someone because we want to feel loved. It has to do with the way we allow ourselves to heal and grow mentally, emotionally, and spiritually to create a space that is essential for our well-being, and that helps us let go of old habits, build our character, and overall become a better person).

In trying to understand the reason why he made me feel like I was unworthy, my heart became hardened. I feared letting someone else close to me. I was disappointed, ashamed, and in regret. I had the intention of having nothing to do with God even when I knew he was the one I needed to be closer to, the one I needed more than anything and anyone else at that moment. But that feeling of knowing I failed Him made me too embarrassed and too disgusted to fall on my face and cry out to Him, to humble myself and pray. I held unforgiveness in my heart because I couldn't understand how someone as good as me could be done so wrong. It opened an emotional and mental wound, and that is what led me to self-harm. I slit my wrist to feel something; as a punishment to myself for being the reason I had gotten heartbroken. I felt like I deserved it, and for the first time in my life, I started to experience something I never thought I'd go through. I felt abandoned, betrayed, forgotten, looked over, and silent in that dark place.

    I lost my identity, trying to be someone else that would fit for a boy who never really deserved me in the first place. I started slacking in school, my relationships with my friends became unimportant to me, and I began to feel like there was no reason for me to live. I felt hopeless, unloved, unappreciated, weak, like *a nobody*. I was scared, unhappy, and tired that I thought the only way out was to take myself out. Everything afterward had been hard for me. I went months without praying to God because I felt like I was too much in my mess for Him to pick me up; I felt *filthy*. But that's the thing I couldn't realize. God never wants to leave us where we are. Whether we're in our mess, or have done things, said things, or thought things that wasn't in His will for us, He loves us deeply to keep us in a place that does not allow our faith to grow during perseverance. He never puts more on us than we can handle. And even though I might have been in the pruning season of my life and thought that it would have killed me (not just physically), I had to learn how to depend and trust in God. I had to accept this season of my life where I had to be okay with not being okay.

    I needed more than just strength. I needed more than just someone telling me that "everything's going to be alright." I was seeking for something that only God could give me in other people. I looked for my worth in them. I looked for love, peace, happiness. I wanted to feel like I was good enough for something, that there was purpose in life, that I meant something to at least someone. Depression is not an easy thing to go through. It takes away your peace of mind and your joy. It's like being arrested and held down by feelings of hopelessness. It's waking up feeling more down than you did before you went to sleep, being a hypocrite of your own emotions, having sleepless nights or sometimes sleeping too much, a loss of appetite, or lack of interest in things that once excited you. It's a horrible feeling to feel like you have no reason to live anymore. The enemy's voice started to taunt me every night, telling me to throw in the towel, that life would be best if I weren't here, that God didn't love me. I kept hearing that this wasn't worth it, that I wasn't supposed to be here in the first place. I felt sick to my stomach, nauseous. His words alone felt like my *crucifixion*.

My spirit was dying, and I needed God the most at that moment. I needed a revival. I knew that I couldn't go through or figure out life without Him, yet I held myself back because I felt so out of reach. I felt too *impure* to be in His presence, and that kept me from asking for His help, His healing, and His guidance. The enemy tried so hard to keep me separated from God that he made me feel guilty for harming myself and for wanting to commit suicide. He made me feel as though it was best not to get help. I strongly encourage you, no matter how you feel, to ask God for help. Even the smallest prayers like "God, I need you," is enough for Him to move on your behalf. There is nothing that could separate you from God or His love (Romans 8:38). Any false burden that you carry, any pain, any regret, any circumstance or trial that you face—things such as depression—please run to God. He will NEVER fail you.

God's spirit will speak words of comfort to you in those dark times. He will say things such as *"Trust me, beloved," "Rest in my bosom." "I will make a way out of no way." "The battle is already won."* When the enemy tries to make you feel defeated, or like there is no hope, God has "given you authority to trample on snakes and scorpions and to overcome all the power of the enemy" (Luke 10:19). You may feel like you may never be happy again, and you might've been stuck in depression way longer than you've hoped, but when you truly understand how much God has placed inside of you, your life will change before your own eyes. When you understand how much your voice matters, how your words can not only shift the way you live but the way you feel inside and out, that spirit of depression and oppression will be shattered.

God will restore, heal, and deliver you from the hands of the enemy. You have the power to overcome depression. You WILL overcome it. You have the power to overcome feelings of shame and unworthiness, heartache, and rejection. God has given you the same ability as Him to call those things into being as though they were not (Romans 4:17 - NIV). You can speak God's word over any situation in your life. You have the willpower to do so because God has placed it inside of you. Those things can and will no longer hold you back from becoming the person that God, since the beginning, has formed you to become. It may seem dark now, but God is saying to you now, no matter how it looks and no matter how it feels, he is standing alongside you. He never lets your cries go unheard. Never.

Points to Ponder:

1. God will NEVER fail you.

2. You have the power to speak God's word over every situation in your life.

3. Luke 10:19 - "I have given you authority to trample on snakes and scorpions and to overcome all the power of the enemy."

A Renewing of The Mind

In John 10:10, the Bible says that the enemy comes to *"steal, kill and destroy."* He comes to steal the joy, the peace, and the stability that God has given you. He comes to steal your desire to pursue everything that you set your mind to; to steal that zeal for prayer and devotion to God. He comes to kill your vision; to make you blind and cause you to think that there will never be anything good coming out of life for you. He tries to blind you from the light at the end of the tunnel, to keep you from walking into the promise that God has ordained for you. And then he comes to destroy your mind. He floods your mentality with unhealthy thinking patterns that will keep you from progressing forward. He strategizes ways to keep you from creating a better version of you, and he fills your mind with negativity to sway you from the truth. If your mind is unstable, the enemy will use this as an advantage to keep you hindered and bring forth oppression. You must renew your mind daily, praying without ceasing and in steadfastness. If you do not guard your mind against destructive thoughts from the enemy, opinions of this world, people, and from yourself, you will always be miserable.

The easiest way for the enemy to have control over you is he starts with your mind first. He understands the power of how it works, and he'll tell you all he can to make you feel less of who God has said that you are. Renewing your mind and keeping your thoughts pure is the hardest thing to do, and it was difficult for me because I had believed lies that shaped me into who I thought I was supposed to be. I wanted to change my image—the image that God had already written out for me—to become a part of an environment and a lifestyle that the Lord says I should be set apart from. I later had to rediscover who I was. I had to become and learn about myself from God's perspective. Renewing your mind is the most crucial part of the entire transformation that God is trying to do in your life. You cannot move forward or think highly of who you are and what you can do if your mind is still tangled in lies and toxic and negative thoughts. You cannot progress with old habits in your mentality. God wants to purify your mind and bring it into subjection of His word and His will.

    My mom once told my siblings and I that "If you don't know who you are, people will label you as someone they want you to be." She was right. I reflected on things I've been told, and I came into an acknowledgment that I was living my life based not only on what I labeled myself as, but on what people and the enemy himself labeled me as. I was living life constructed on words that I believed until I came into my truth. I had to remove that identity that they've given me—that I've given myself and declare the word of God over my mind, my heart, and my spirit.

    Do not allow people to weaken you with their poor self-image of how they *see* you. How they decide to accept and perceive you is their problem, not yours. Your words are effective, and you must remember that life and death lie in the power of your tongue (Proverbs 18:21). You must continuously speak positively to yourself, even when you feel anything but positive. The enemy is the Father of lies; he can't and never will tell the truth. Anything that he has claimed you to be, you are the complete opposite. If he said that you are a failure, proclaim that you are an overcomer because that is who God has said you are. If he whispered in your spirit that you are ugly, begin to pray Psalm 139:13-14. "For you created my inmost being; you knit me together in my mother's womb. I praise you because *I am fearfully and wonderfully made*; your works are wonderful; I know that full well." (emphasis added).

    You are beautiful in the eyesight of God, and when you lose yourself or forget who and what God has called, read through the scripture. Doing this will help you grow a more profound and intimate relationship with Him. It will guide you into prayer and communion with Him and He will begin to reveal and give you clarity of who you are in Him. His truth will blow your mind. You are ambitious, you are worth it, and you are strong. God has created you wonderfully, and you are pleasing in His eyes. The only thing that should ever matter in life is what God says about you. A boy does not define your worth, and this world does not get to tell you who you should be and how you should look. Don't let words of others tear you down. You are God's *masterpiece*, His art.

Do not conform to this world. You are different. It's okay to look, to talk, to have opposite beliefs and standards from your peers. Be happy with the person you are, even when you don't fit in with everyone else around you. To boost your self-esteem and break off insecure strongholds, here are a few affirmations that I've written down and spoken over myself. You can pray these affirmations or simply speak these over yourself whenever you feel at your lowest.

Affirmations When You're Feeling Worthless:

- "I am worth it."
- "I have value in God."
- "I am more than enough."
- "Because God loves me with an everlasting love, I know that I am a precious jewel."
- "I am a royal priesthood."

Affirmations When You're Feeling Ugly:

- "I am fearfully and wonderfully made in God's image."
- "I am the apple of God's eye."
- "I am beautiful."
- "I was created to be different."
- "God makes no mistakes because he is the perfect potter and I am his clay."
- "I am a wonderful work in Christ."

Affirmations When You Feel Like Giving Up:

- "I can do all things through Christ who strengthens me."
- "Everything is possible with God."
- "I will stand firm in my faith and be courageous and strong."
- "I know that sometimes I will fall, but God will always be there to pick me up."

Affirmations When You Lack Confidence in Yourself:

- "God's love makes me complete."
- "God is within me."
- "God is doing a great work in me."
- "I have confidence in myself because I know that the Lord is always by my side."
- "I have confidence because I trust in God."
- "I am strong, powerful and worthy in Christ."

Affirmations When You're Feeling Depressed:

- "I will think of things that are pure, and just, and upright and lovely."
- "Because God is always with me, I will not be afraid."
- "I am not alone."
- "God will never leave me nor forsaken me."
- "God will hear my cry and deliver me."
- "The Lord is my healer and my comforter."
- "Because I know that God cares for me, I will place my anxiety in his hands."
- "God is the Prince of Peace."

These are a few that you could use daily, or you could write down your own and read through scripture on anything you are having an issue facing. I pray in hope that this will help you find your strength and identity in Christ as it did with me.

Points to Ponder:

1. Renew your mind daily.

2. Do not let this world tell you who you should be.

3. Be and walk in your identity in Christ.

Speak and write down affirmations. Believe them. Live them.

Coming into A New Image

When I started walking in the belief of God's truth, when I continually feed myself with His word and accepted my flaws, I noted changes in my life and great progress in my mentality. Those old labels were ripped off, and instantly, I felt replenished; I felt rejuvenated. When I looked in the mirror, I no longer felt disgusted by what was staring back at me. Daily, I felt God's love for me as I made a commitment to myself that I was going to pursue God the best way I knew how. Although I've had days where I felt down, I found my strength in prayer. Being humble and allowing God to uplift you when you feel like you're getting weak and pursuing Him and building a meaningful relationship is one of the best feelings in the world.

    When you start applying God's word in your life and believing everything that He says about you, you will be transformed and grow internally as well as externally. However, healing from my heartbreak was still a process. There were some things I couldn't seem to let it go of. At times, I found myself stuck in the past, and I had to realize if I wanted to move forward, I had to unloose myself from the strongholds of my past. The Bible says in Psalm 34:18 that "the Lord is close to the brokenhearted and saves those who are crushed in spirit." I allowed myself to become unidentifiable with what I was told, what I've experienced and started identifying myself with things that I've learned about who I am in God. The lessons I've learned through my darkest trial is what made me discover who I was in Christ.

As I received the healing God wanted for me, I accepted my hurt and no longer blamed it on the one who caused it. I unvictimized myself and had taken full responsibility for ignoring the red flags that God had been showing me. Once I released those feelings of bitterness, anger, hatred, and disgust I had against the boy who damaged my spirit, God instantly gave me peace within myself. I forgave him sincerely for what he's done and was able to move forward. One truth I learned was that if I didn't dedicate my time to knowing who God is, I would know fully who I am. A piece of who He is lives in us, we are made in His image. If you haven't fully dedicated your time to know who God truly is, how would you expect to know who you really are?
Your entire well-being is the creator's work. God knows you better than you know yourself. The scripture says in Jeremiah 1:5, "before you were formed in the womb, God knew you and set you apart. Allow God to fully shift you and your life around for good; for His good. The process of change from the things you're familiar with won't always feel good or be easy, but it'll be worth it.

When you know who and whose you are, anything that people speak against you will no longer affect you mentally or emotionally because you'll be able to stand firm and believe in God and His word. You will be able to discern the voice of the enemy from God's and stand against your own beliefs with the knowledge and wisdom of your identity in Christ. Having a renewed mind and spirit is like crucifying your old self— your old way of thinking, your old way of talking, your old way of doing things. And when you find out who you are, you are a new creature in God. You're a new person, built stronger, mentally, emotionally, and spiritually.

It's important to keep yourself grounded in God's word, to understand and be authentic to who you are without feeling an urge to change your appearance for someone to choose you, like you, or want you. When you find confidence in God, living your life according to the belief that you are fearfully and wonderfully made, worthy, an overcomer, and that you have authority, you will feel more like the person God has made you to be. Accepting the things that I wanted to change but couldn't was very hard for me to do because I wanted to be perfect. Once I fell in love with my skin, and every imperfection that shaped me into who I am, the thought of even wanting to look like anyone else became vague. It took a while for me to believe that I was beautiful because my heart was scarred from the rejection and not knowing my worth. When God began to show me myself through His eyes, He gave me revelation pertaining to me. I knew my value, and I was not going to force anyone else to see how much I was worth.

Points to Ponder:

1. Be accepting of the things you cannot change about yourself.

2. Jeremiah 1:5 - "Before I formed you in the womb, I knew you, before you were born, I set you apart."

3. You have the authority to speak life over yourself.

Knowing Who You Are in God

Often, when we've been rejected or betrayed by people, by those you've felt comfortable being vulnerable with, unknowingly we tend to place the same characteristics and standards of a human being onto God when He is the total opposite. You can't put God in a box, expecting Him to be the same as what you've seen in the natural. Why? Because He is a God who never changes, who never fails. His character is of good and not of evil. You must believe it in your heart that you'll never feel abandoned or forsaken in dark times. The Bible says in Matthew 28:20 that God will be with you always even to the very end. No matter what circumstances you may face, no matter if you feel alone, take God at His word and know that He's always there for you.

When you know who you are in God, you'll always feel peace and security within yourself. You'll be happy being you, accepting of the things you can and cannot change and knowing that you are unique. You'll never have this feeling of wanting to be like anyone else but who God has made you to be.

Your self-esteem and character will be built upon the foundation of God's truth, and you will be able to pull down every vain imagination, every false thought that you've had about yourself and God. You were not created to follow and uphold standards based on what the world tells you to do. You were created to be and walk in the purpose and the lifestyle that God has already written out for your life. Do not corrupt your true self-image trying to fit the mold of this world, but instead grasp ahold to God's word and be confident in your identity.

When your identity is firmly rooted in Christ, you will never feel pressured to meet someone else's expectations of who they want you to be. When you find your mind becoming clouded with negative thoughts, meditate on God's word and remember your identity in Him. Use scripture and affirmations to help uplift your spirit. Here are a few statements along with the correlating scriptures that you could use every day to keep you in remembrance of who you are and whose you are as well as help you fight against negative thinking.

- I am complete in God. (Colossians 2:10)

- I am a royal priesthood. (1 Peter 2:9)

- God knew me before He formed me in my mother's womb. He has set me apart. (Jeremiah 1:5)

- I am more than a conqueror. (Romans 8:37)

- I am fearfully and wonderfully made. (Psalm 139:14)

- I am the image of God. (Genesis 1:27)

- Because God is within me, I will not fall. (Psalm 46:5)

- I am confident in knowing that God is working all things (every experience, every hurt, every trial or tribulation) together for my good. (Romans 8:28)

- I'm not afraid because I know that God is with me wherever I go. (Joshua 1:9)

- I find my strength in Christ. (Isaiah 41:10)

- Although I may go through dark and hard times in my life, I will not be fearful because I know that God is with me, and He is my comfort. (Psalm 23:4)

- I am God's masterpiece. (Ephesians 2:10)

- I was chosen by Christ, in Christ. (Ephesians 1:11)

- God's peace will guard my heart and mind. (Philippians 4:7)

- I am victorious. (Romans 21:7)

- I may feel alone sometimes, but I know that God will never leave me nor forsake me. (Hebrews 13:5)

Meditate on these things and hide them in your heart. Just knowing what the Word of God says has helped me walk in my truth and have confidence in myself. It helped heal and transform me; it changed my entire perception of myself and allowed me to boldly grow and become the person God created me to be. My relationship with God became more consistent; my hunger and thirst for more of God increased daily.

    I am a completely new person in God, and this is all I'll ever want to be. My life changed when God revealed Himself to me. I'd wake up and no longer feel bound or emotional; I no longer felt numb or insecure, no longer felt pressured to become like anyone else. My spirit became strengthened when I felt God consume me with love, security, peace, joy, healing, and comfort. As I pushed myself to build a relationship with Christ, He has done nothing but shown himself faithful in my life. And because of Him, I can be comfortable and happy in my skin. The best thing to be is the person God has made you to be and walking in who He says you are in Him. His word is truth, and it's your strength when you feel like you have none.

You are valuable and accepted by God. Don't allow anyone to make you feel less than. Be you even when the world says otherwise, even when your friends try to change your character, or when it seems hard to fit in with a group. You were called to stand out and be different; be unique. There is so much that comes with you acknowledging who you are in Christ, so much power that you gain with wisdom He gives. Often, Satan tries to keep you from finding yourself in God because he knows the moment you find your identity in the one who is the creator of all things (Colossians 1:16), he can no longer damage the way you see and feel about yourself.

Points to Ponder:

1. God is NOT like man.

2. You are more than who people say you are.

3. God's word is truth.

Knowing Who God Is

No matter how many times you've failed at something, no matter how many times you've been in doubt, found yourself sinking into depression, wanting to throw in the towel, or belittled yourself, you are a conqueror, you are valuable, beautiful, strong and important to God. You are fearlessly bold, and you stand out. You are YOU, and only God's word can truly define who you are because he has the final say pertaining to everything in your life.

Walk in faith and in the joy of the Lord. There may be times when you doubt; when you lose hope; when you start to feel like there isn't a way out, that you'll never be happy, times when you feel unworthy. I've been there. But one thing I know for sure is that no matter what I was feeling, no matter how many times I've felt alone, misunderstood, rejected, taken for granted, lost, and dead inside; God always showed up during my situation.

I felt Him speak to my heart plenty of times, just telling me that He was there and not to be afraid, not to be anxious for nothing. He used people to prophesy an encouraging word to me. He spoke life to my wounded spirit and purified not only my mind but my heart from bitterness. I was able to forgive those who've hurt me because I knew who I was, and the promises God made to me. I am in a better place mentally, emotionally, and spiritually, but I still speak life over myself.

Every label that has been placed underneath my name, the things people expected me to be, or wanted me to be, God removed the labels and gave me a new and perfect image. I no longer lived up to the expectations of others. I stopped living my life trying to be someone that I wasn't just to be accepted and noticed by people who don't matter.

People will think and say whatever they can just to damage you, but if you know the truth in the word of God and live it out daily, every word that has been spoken or will be spoken over your life will fall at your feet. You will learn and enjoy being who you are when you know God. He makes *no mistakes,* and if you've ever felt like you were a mistake, I am here to tell you that you aren't. God created you exactly how He wanted you to be, how He saw you. You are perfect in his eyes, flaws and all.

Because I am rooted in Christ, and I now know who I am in Him, whenever I start to feel like I do not measure up to an expectation which I feel I have to meet for other people, I remind myself that putting God and His word first will have everything else fall into place. I use a method that helps me remember who He says that I am. In this method, I write a statement starting with the mention of my name and simply fill in the blank with the truth of who I know I am in God.

Here's my example:

My name is Amayah, and I am the image of God. Doing this allows me to walk, talk, and become more like God, to live a life that is pleasing to Him and not others. It removes the pressure of what society makes us believe we should become.

I encourage you to try this as well so that you can be reminded of how much you are valued, seen, and loved. You are not defined by what you do or who you've told yourself you were going to turn out to be. The word of God defines you.

Knowing who we are in God determines how well we know Him. We will never be able to be our authentic selves in the full potential that God wants us to be if we don't fully know who God Himself is. These are a few Scriptures that'll help remind you of who Christ is just as it helped me when I journeyed to find out who I was in God.

- He is gracious, righteous, and full of compassion. (Psalm 116:5)

- He is love. (1 John 4:8)

- He is a merciful God. (Deuteronomy 4:31)

- He is strength, salvation, powerful, holy, awesome in glory, a redeemer, a God of unfailing love, a warrior, a God who shatters the enemy, a God who works wonders. (Exodus 15.1-6)

- He is the way, the truth, and the life. (1 John 14:6)

- He is the Alpha and the Omega, the First and the Last, the Beginning and the End. (Revelation 22:13)

- He is a God of faithfulness and without iniquity. (Deuteronomy 32:4)

- He is "I am who I am." (Exodus 3:14)

- He is the God of the impossible. (Luke 18:27)

- He is the creator of the heavens and the earth. (Genesis 1:1)

- He is a God who forgives. (1 John 1:9)

- He is the everlasting God. (Isaiah 40:28)

- He is Lord, the maker of all things. (Isaiah 44:24)

- He is good, a refuge in times of trouble. (Nahum 1:7)

Points to Ponder:

1. Know God for who He is.

2. There is truth in God's word.

3. God made no mistake when He created you.

A New Truth

In God's eyes, we are liberated, loved, and redeemed for who we are. Instead of trying to figure out how people view us and what they think about us, the only thing that is important for you to know is what God thinks of you. In the book of Isaiah 41:1, we are reminded that God has called us by name and that we are His. He shapes us into His perfect image just as a potter does clay.

Question Reflection:

- Are the things that people say you are falling in line with who God says that you are?

- Who do you know God to be?

- Are you more concerned about what people think of you or what God thinks of you?

- What words are you speaking over yourself?

- Do you believe God at his Word?

- How can you help others find themselves in God?

The truth about who we are in Christ is all in His word. I'm amazed at how much I've learned about myself. It was the best turn around God could have ever done in my life. I was in awe of the way he thought of me, and I couldn't believe how long it took for me to realize that the answers I was looking for were right underneath my nose. I searched for myself in my friends and tried to find myself in a boy when all I could've done was search in God. I experienced a feeling of joy and fulfillment when God brought clarity to me. He washed me clean and loved me unconditionally, despite how many times I've failed Him. I used to be this girl who had trouble looking at herself in the mirror and picked at her nails because she hated what she saw. I used to be this girl who wanted to feel important to someone outside of family; a girl who ran after someone who couldn't value her. I was a broken, scared, and scarred girl.

But I found my light in Christ. I found my hope and my strength, my faith, and my healing in Him. I let Him engulf me with His presence, and I was willing to accept change even though it made me uncomfortable. I found my identity in God, and I know that you can too. You are worth it. You are special and powerful; you are important and seen, loved, valued, strong, and beautiful in God. You are a conqueror; you are wise, fearless, and confident. Live in the truth of God.

Know that you are the opposite of every bad word spoken to you and continue to read God's word. Your life will change, and you will see the goodness of God and understand that His love for you is like no other. You will have a hunger for Him, and you will live out your purpose because you know who you are. Everything that you used to feel about yourself will fade away because God has given you the perfect image. Despite what society says you should look like, dress like, or talk like, you will find peace in being different; in being a leader. You will no longer feel left out or out of place; instead, you will stand out and draw other people to lead them to Christ. I want to give you a few prayers on specific things I've dealt with on the journey to finding myself, and I pray that this inspires you to either write your own or simply pray these whenever times get tough.

<u>Prayer for Strength:</u>

Lord, I kneel to you as humble as I know how, asking that you give me mental, emotional, and spiritual strength. I pray in faith that you will meet me in my muck and uplift my broken spirit. I am yielded to you, God, knowing that you will hear my cry and answer my prayer. Because I know that I find strength in you, that you are the strength that I need, I am asking that you allow it to flow through me. I am no longer weak but made strong in you. Thank you for being my strength. Thank you for drawing your hand to help me stand again. You are within me, and I will not fall. I receive it in your son, Jesus' name, Amen.

Prayer for Confidence:

Lord be my confidence and keep my foot from being caught. Help me to stand in knowing that you are with me and live within me. I pray that there will be a boost in my self-confidence and that I am receptive to the revelation that you will reveal concerning who I am in you. I release my cares upon you, praying and believing that I will no longer be pressured or bound by false burden. You are my confidence; let it shine outwardly. In Jesus' name, Amen.

Prayer for Healing:

Lord, I am broken and in shame. Because you are a healing God, I come to you seeking a powerful delivery in my heart, my mind, and my spirit. I pray that you consume me and remove any deep wound and allow me to walk in my healing. Teach me to let go of things I can control and accept the things I can't change. Your words say that by your stripes (wounds) we are healed. Thank you, God, for your healing power, thank you for the healing of your blood. In Jesus' name, Amen.

Prayer for Destroying Insecurity:

Lord, endow me with your spirit and remove every label I've placed upon myself. The things that I've thought negatively towards myself, I pull those strongholds down and replace them with who you say that I am. Continue to reveal myself to me and speak to my heart. Everything that the enemy has subjected me as, I bind and rebuke those lies in the name of Jesus, and I stand firm in knowing who and whose I am. Your word is my truth, and I will live through it and live by it. I will be who you've created me to be. I am the image and likeness of God. I am fearfully and wonderfully made in you. I am beautiful. I will no longer live up to the expectation of being perfect or be concerned by the thoughts of other people. Your word has the final say, and I will walk in my true, authentic, rich self-image in Jesus' name, Amen.

Everything that I've gone through was for God's purpose in my life. I had to lose myself so that I could find my identity in God. I had to experience my first heartbreak, so I could run back to my first love; so, I could find and be loved by Him. I had to be beaten down, pushed over, spiritually broken, and weak, so I could find hope, strength, faith, and restoration in Him. He gave me everything I was seeking, and I hadn't understood why things started to go left for me. But the scripture tells me in John 13:7 "Jesus replied, 'you do not realize now what I am doing, but later you will understand.'" And I understand now.

He gives each one of us a story to tell, some different than others. The most traumatizing parts of your life, the most shameful and ugly parts are the parts that will not only bring you healing but help free someone else. Yes, I second-guessed writing this because I knew I had to feel vulnerability, I had to think about things I wanted to forget, I had to become uncomfortable and open, to cry again. Thoughts were going through my head: *"This won't be good enough," "You shouldn't have written this."* But I knew that was the enemy trying to stop me from sharing my truth. Through revisiting my past, God was removing things from me in the inside; He was healing me and revealing the true me. He was giving me my life and my identity back.

As I've mentioned before, you are everything God has said in His word about you. Never let anyone tell you who you should be or let them make you doubt your ability, you can do everything through God. You are somebody, even with the mistakes, the faults, and the flaws. Remember that God is there with you through it all. He loves and cares for you deeply. You are more than who you think you are; *you are who God says you are.*

Points to Ponder:

1. You are somebody, even with your flaws.

2. You are fearfully and wonderfully made.

3. You are ONLY who God says you are.

Conclusion

In conclusion, everything that you've thought yourself to be or everything that others have told you that you were is not your reality. There is so much more to you than what you think, and God is willing to reveal all that you are in Him if you'll allow yourself to submit underneath His words about who you are and how you should live your life in Him. Although it's not easy sometimes, you must understand that there is a God who cares about you. When you feel alone, know that He's there. When you are confused, he is your clarity. When you feel unheard, He listens. When you feel lost, He is your direction.

No matter how this world tries to convince you that things are better if you live by their standard, God's way for your life is far greater than anything society tries to sway you with. You are someone special, don't devalue your worth because someone doesn't appreciate you for who God has made you to be. Trust in the process that God has for your life and hold onto his unchanging hand. You may not understand the reason behind things you go through, but everything doesn't last forever, and God never puts you in situations He knows you aren't able to handle. The enemy will always try to magnify your insecurities and lead you to doubt what God says about you. He understands that the moment you know who and whose you are, he is incapable of pulling you away from God. He will try to use your insecurities as bondage to not only ruin your relationship with the Heavenly Father but with your family and friends also.

Every void that you feel, God's word will bring you revelation, clarity, and restoration. It will give you freedom from the bondage of words people have spoken over you, the lies that the enemy has told you, and the things that you've said to yourself. You are NOT your past mistakes or bad choices. You are beautiful and created in the image of God. You are NOT a mistake but a masterpiece. You are **EVERYTHING** and **ONLY** who God says you are.

"For we are God's masterpiece. He has created us anew in Christ Jesus, so we can do the good things He planned for us long ago." (Ephesians 2:10 NLT – New Living Translation)

Amayah Shantel Smith

is an author and emerging leader from Houston, Texas. She is on fire for God and is on a mission to inspire, motivate and transform the next generation of young girls. Amayah has won the battle in her mind as she struggled with finding her identity, security, and purpose. She lives by Psalm 139:14; *"I praise you because I am fearfully and wonderfully made, your works are wonderful, I know that full well."*

In her own transformation in finding identity in Christ, she knew that in order to be an effective witness she must share her testimony to reach the hearts of other teenage girls that share similar experiences that she has overcome. Her desire is to inspire and bring hope to teenage girls across the globe by reassuring them that they are **BEAUTIFULLY AND WONDERFULLY MADE**. Her prayer is that the words of her book, "Who Does God Say You Are?" will be light and saving grace for those who need it most.

Amayah is the recipient of the Miss S.H.I.N.E. (Serve Him in Everything) award. She is noted amongst others as being inspirational. Although young, Amayah is powerful and is changing many lives in her generation and beyond. She is a talented individual who enjoys empowering others and singing God's praises as a praise and worship leader at The Mouth of God Ministries. Amayah enjoys reading, journaling, spending time with family and singing. She is loved and supported by her parents, Fentress and LaShundra Smith and her 11 siblings.

www.ingramcontent.com/pod-product-compliance
Lightning Source LLC
LaVergne TN
LVHW051201080426
835508LV00021B/2743